"In the collection of poems, Laura opens the door for all of us to see beyond our limits and losses to an expansive world of love and possibility. As great writers do, Laura puts words to things that you might not be able to name for yourself, and brings us all to the greatest strength we have in this life — hope."

Nicole Unice, pastor, counselor, and author of several books, including her latest, *The Struggle is Real*

"Laura's pen bleeds honesty and a viscous clinging to hope. Her life and writings are an inspiration to us all. Read, and be moved..."

Rex Alphin, author of *The Nature of Things* and *Lamentations of a Son*

"Author Gregg Levoy writes, 'In stone sculpting, an artist taps a stone lightly with a hammer to see if it's 'true.' If it emits a dull tone, it has faults running through it that will crack it apart when you work on it. A clear ring, one that hangs in the air for a moment, means it's true, has integrity, and most importantly, will hold up under repeated blows.' *Beyond* is a collection of captivating poems that send a clear ring. Each line, each word, lingering in the air of our thoughts for a moment, inviting us to pause, ponder, and process the deeper places – the ones often visited 'out of sight' where there is 'no one to see or ask why' (*Weeping Willow*). Laura carefully and thoughtfully allows us to journey through the four movements of limits, longings, love, and loss with her and, in doing so, calls us forward into living a life that 'will hold up under repeated blows' – a life that faces pain and presses through to the peace and power waiting on the other side."

Janell Rardon, therapist and author of *Overcoming Hurtful Words: Rewrite Your Own Story*

"Laura has truly done something that most poets aspire to but few ever actually achieve. In her book she manages to bring the reader into her own experience of disability while allowing her poetry to gently and firmly open the reader to a better understanding of their own journey. Although Laura's framework is largely faith-based in nature, the experiences she recounts are so universal and so authentically told, that anyone who reads this will discover new things about themselves through her poetry."

Rev. Justin Hancock, lead pastor and co-founder of The Julian Way, a ministry for persons with disabilities

"Laura shares her unique story in a novel way through poetry. You feel her story, her experience, rather than simply being told about it. She provides deep, at times raw, yet also beautiful glimpses into her life."

Jeff McNair, director of Church Relations for Joni and Friends' Christian Institute on Disability (CID)

"Laura has written a short collection of even shorter poems, but don't be fooled by their brevity. They are powerful in the ways they capture moments, moments in long processes, moments that call for you to stop your quick read and remember the ways her moments speak to yours. Like flashes of light that let you see into a darkness or gloom, they cannot be captured, but can help you see the path behind, the place you are, and the way ahead. Honest, poignant, painful, hopeful, Laura shows us you don't need a lot of words to capture what it means to be human. Read them, and hope you get the opportunity to hear her read them in person."

Bill Gaventa, author, speaker, consultant, and founder of Institute on Theology and Disability

Beyond

limits. longings. love. loss.

a collection of poems

Laura C. Robb

Printed in the United States of America

First Printing, 2019
ISBN 978-1-54399-279-3

BookBaby Publishing
7905 N. Crescent Blvd.
Pennsauken, NJ 08110

www.LauraCRobb.com

To
the family I grew up with
the friends I have gained
you are my people
my community
Home

you move me beyond
every day
life is better together
always

this book
the first

For
You

Contents

Loss

Foreword

The book you hold in your hands is the result of several years of interior work by a dear friend of mine.

Laura and I first met in 1994 when my family moved to her hometown, not long before her tenth birthday, to which I was invited. Thus began years of laughter, sleepovers, trips to Dairy Queen, youth retreats, and floating on inner tubes at our local pool in the hot Virginia sun. But our friendship has also been one of sharing our interior lives: our thoughts and dreams, our fears and failures. Sadly, it can be difficult to come by such a friendship; we have enjoyed ours for twenty-five years now.

For nearly ten years, we have shared poetry. Before anyone else knew that she (or I) wrote poems, we held each other's secret. As Laura puts it in the Preface, poetry is where we went "to understand." And thankfully, we went there together.

We both came to poetry in grief. She, at the beginning of a series of deaths in her family, and I, at the loss of a special friendship. We found a measure of healing in the articulation, something soothing in the craft, in the careful attention to words. We found a new way to pray.

It is an old way, of course, when we realize the Psalms are first of all poems. They are poems full of fear, anger, confusion, and questions right alongside praise, elation, confidence, and joy — all offered to God. Laura's poems are filled with no less!

It is an honor to be invited into her first book of interior-made-exterior: a small record of a season of one woman's becoming. Her psalm-like lines, while often sparse and with no fear of white space, carry in them her devotion as well as her honest wrestling. The two are not mutually exclusive, as David, Asaph, and the rest knew.

In this first collection of her poetry, Laura is a good guide, inviting us to consider our own laments and hopes. May her pilgrimage through and beyond limits, longings, love, and loss shine a light on your own journey.

Anna A. Friedrich
poet, speaker, & staff worker at L'Abri Fellowship

Preface

I couldn't ignore it.

The sudden absence.
The abrupt ending.
The hole in my heart.

Grief.

I've been here before and I was back.

The silence and space screamed. Reminders of my loss were everywhere. I couldn't ignore grief this time. I had to go deeper. I let loss do what only loss can do, if we allow it.

One grieving season led me on a path I never expected. It was the beginning of a series of losses.

Losses come in many forms. It can be the death of a loved one, the death of a relationship, or the death of a dream. All loss signals an unwanted goodbye.

Loss can force us to ask hard questions, like… *Why, God? How long will it hurt? How do I thrive again?*

Mixed in with the grief I found another emotion.

Anger.

Loss makes room for anger. It can allow us to be honest about the pain.

We might miss the person who left, the dream that shattered.

We long for the unmet, the unspoken.

We crave the love we don't have.

We question where we've been and where we're going because we want more. We know what could be.

And if you're like me, sometimes we want the unreachable, impossible dreams for ourselves.

Beyond is about endings that lead to new and unexpected beginnings. It is about learning to recognize the limits we cannot erase, the longings we carry, the love we crave, and the losses that change us.

Beyond is also a journey of wrestling.

> Of accepting disability.
> Of admitting dreams.
> Of loving and losing.

> Mostly it is about *being, becoming*, and *seeing beyond*.

Throughout the book, I tell my story and I invite you to explore your own. Each section ends with a question for you to ponder. Take your time with the reading of the poems and the reflecting of your story. As you walk through what I have experienced, maybe you will relate to pieces of my journey or connect with some of my struggles.

Limits look like weaknesses to the world. We come to the end of our ability and the beginning of something greater than us, a strength from the One who made us.

Longings can be difficult to admit. Mine stayed hidden for years. Naming our longings and bringing them to the light is the end of isolation and the beginning of inclusion.

Love is always a risk. However, love carries the potential for profound gifts. Within a relationship, we can know the end of loneliness and the beginning of belonging at the deepest level.

Loss means we have loved. And if we have loved, we have lived well. It is the end of what was a present reality and the beginning of what is now a treasured past.

If you are in a grieving season, don't rush to the other side. Loss is simultaneously wrapped in the hard and the happy. We wonder how we can move on to what is next while we remember what we had.

Honoring the grieving season is what carried me to find the door of Hope again.

Poetry is where I go for the unspeakable, the unexplainable. It's where I go to understand.

May each poem lead you to –

somewhere you've been,
somewhere you are, or
somewhere you hope to go.

Limits

STIFLING THE SWEET SELF

the world around me stares
not quite knowing what to say
young ones and old, all have spoken
strange words, words of unawares
words that speak deeply to me
revealing the heart of their soul

such moments I do recall
from my earlier years
stifling the sweet self
but I have come to understand
how those awkward words
brought a new strength
burning a desire to lay bare
what is behind my blue eyes
and under this red hair

TRAPPED

today

I am trapped
waiting to be
free

I am fragmented
piecing together
me

I am absent
hoping to
return

I am laden
with words that
burn

I am jumbled
looking for
time

tomorrow

FRUSTRATED

frustrated
I find no time
I see no sign
stuck in a rut

the hours go by
and I try, I try
tasks undone but
another day ends

I am home
yet feel alone
what can I do?
where are you?

inside I shut
my soul closes up
wanting
to escape
even if brief
hoping
for a moment
a season of relief

CHASING A MYSTERY

a foggy brain, a blank mind
somewhere I left me
somewhere I cannot find
all I know is how I feel
this new self is not real
creativity gone, thoughts unclear
I am still here, I am still here
under the cloud, so very near
somewhere I left me
chasing a mystery

THE STORY TO TELL

wheelchair, walker
with the help of a hand
I go places and do things
as much as I can
this disability I have
these limits you see
yes, they're a challenge
but not one to stop me

     love life
     live it well
          that's the story
        I have to tell

IMPOSSIBLE IS NOT A WORD

impossible is not a word
not one I often choose
giving up is un-preferred
for it means to fail, to lose
and that, to me, is absurd
when I can easily embrace
a different view, a new word

UNKNOWN ANSWERS

How long shall I stay? Who will say?
Will you show me the way?
Do I think of a plan, wait for a man
or decide what to do when I think I can?
For what do I wait? Why do I hope?
How much longer can I cope?
What age will I be? When will I see?
Who will continue to care for me?
Does anyone know? Can you understand
these questions, my heart, my fears
that rise to the surface unplanned?

BEYOND

more than you think
beyond what you see
disabled is not
      my identity

I'm Laura
a person
of value
worth
dignity
another member
      of humanity

See Beyond

Facing and embracing our limits allows us to learn valuable lessons, such as relying on God and others.

Consider one of your limits. What can that limit teach you?

Longings

SIMPLE DREAMS

simple dreams I long to do
instead I must rely on you
or try to change my point of view

take a trip, drive a car
visit friends who live afar
cook a meal, do my hair
have no need for a wheelchair
ride a bike, run a mile
take friends' kids for a while
reach a book, live on my own
have extended time alone
walk barefoot, wear other shoes
leave town whenever I choose

such things I can only dream
waiting for the One to redeem

IMAGINE WHAT COULD BE

imagine what could be
wait for what to see
live the story of me

God has plans, ideas
of who I could
       should
       will be

imagine what is past
   where I've been
imagine what's in store
   where I'm headed
      which door?

what's in the future?
around the next bend?
He knows what's coming
what lingers just ahead

today is here, today I have
tomorrow is tomorrow
imagine what could be

WHERE

not there
here is where I am
longing to be

where
life is pleasant
love is grand

where
I do not falter
I only stand

where
strongly I stand
for what is true

where
I cling simply to You

THE WAR WITHIN

wage
> the war within

rage
> against the sin

stage
> the heart to begin

disengage
turn the page
fight to win

BE

slow down
look up
let yourself

    be

    awake

    alive

    abundantly free

let go
hold on
watch and see

STORMS

clouds cover the earth
hiding the light of the sun
troubles consume the joy within
afflictions rain down

for a season

remember, recall
eventually
the storm will fall

fall apart

the earth shakes
the wind blows

stirred

renewed, refreshed
different than before
clouds lift to reveal
the sky once more

DOUBT

thoughts pouring in

words
leaking

out

wondering when

beginning
to

doubt

MOUNTAINS

life brings
steep hills
mountains
to climb

find
a path
the way
to go

slow
and steady
gradually up
up to the top

stop

obstacles
conquered

BELONG

wait
    hope
        search
            for a place
            that space
            to feel
            accepted
            understood
            loved

            time
            needed

            be open
            grow
            meet
            learn
            know
            welcome

            embrace
            time

            find

            belong

STAY

dreams
just out of reach
dreams
where I want to be
teach
      me to stay
            stay
     stay right here
stop looking
        ahead
        away
        stay
where you are
home

See Beyond

We all have longings. Some we carry quietly for a
time, not wanting to name what is in our hearts.

Simple or impossible, what do you hope for?

Love

DEAR FRIEND

I cannot hide
you know me so well
in you I confide
to you I tell
my hopes and fears
with smiles and tears

thank you, dear friend
for a love with no end

CONVERSATIONS AT COFFEE SHOPS

conversations at coffee shops
sipping sweet drinks
savoring scents
hearing machines
muffled mellow music

lingering in time
two treasured friends

engaging wishful wants
    delicate desires
wasting no words
    over worry
    or willful woes
sharing simple sorrows
    avid ambitions

       listening
        learning

           to live and love well

for such a fleeting flash
　　　　　all life stops

WAKE UP

your face
your eyes
your smile
that look
I miss
that spark
I hope
to see

catch
one
more
glimpse
even if
even if
you are
real
only
in my dreams

is it wrong?
can I ask?
when will we
you and I
be friends?

wake up
wake up
to reality

MAYBE I READ IN BETWEEN

I've seen the way you look at me
and heard the words you said
I thought I was correct to think
you might like me in return
but maybe I read in between
and told my heart what to see

I've wanted to deny how I feel
the joy, the strength, the hope
of just having you around
because every day I've been afraid
that maybe I read in between
and none of this is real

WAITING

I won't let go
I need to know

do you think
do you feel
what I hold
in my heart
waiting to reveal?

WHAT I THOUGHT I KNEW

I see without feeling what I thought I knew
every moment each time I would see you
am I still hoping? do I even wait?
I must confess: you did not stir
these affections, these longings
my deep down desires that were
yet have I moved on? is it too late
to wonder, to look for a hint or a taste?
again I dream, I only want to pursue
the idea that you, or someone I meet
will simply be open to loving me too

YOU SEE ME

there's something about you
something I can't always describe
something I just know deep inside

accepted, protected
gathered, connected
I felt these from the start
but I hesitated, is this real?
what is happening right now?

I don't understand why or how
how are you so comfortable?

you know I have limits
you know I need help
you're more than aware
yet you see me
not disability or the chair
you see me

there's something about you
I could tell from the start
but I hesitated, is this real?
should I, could I, can I?

See Beyond

Through our relationships, we are changed.
We learn to receive and reciprocate love.

How has the experience of love deepened your life?

Loss

LOST IN A DREAM

my heart is heavy and I am lost in a dream
nothing in life is quite what it seems
we come to a point or period of time
where it feels we are losing more than we gain

there is still hope in my life, a small subtle sign
that all is not lost -- pockets of joy I see in the pain
these moments carry me through the quiet days
as waves of sadness come crashing in my soul

I cannot predict, but I see hints of yesterday
when loved ones were here and physically whole
now there is an emptiness that I can only fill
with the beautiful memories I treasure still

I look to the future and in the depth of my heart
I ache for the love lost, for the love I long to impart

WHEN THE DAY MEETS THE NIGHT

When the Day is silent and the hour is four
the phone isn't ringing and you're not at the door
Something is missing that I cannot ignore
You are gone
You are with us no more

Who will fill this empty hole? Who can I call?
How long must we feel the effects of the Fall?

When the hour is seven and the Day meets the Night
we wait every Sunday for the phone to light
Is anyone on the line? No, not quite
You have left
You are now out of our sight

Who will fill this empty hole? Who can I call?
How long must we feel the effects of the Fall?

When the time is festive and all gather for the Day
the family is smaller, but we still look your way
We remember and share stories of yesterday
You moved on
You went ahead and away

Who will fill this empty hole? Who can I call?
How long must we feel the effects of the Fall?

SISTER

a name so familiar, yet I never knew
the face in the photo staring back at you
a sister we once had before we were born
two short years and then she was torn
away from this life, far from here
one day I'll meet you, one day, one year

THE DREAM DOOR

the dream door
opened quickly
    something new
       to explore
    the heart soared
    even in sorrow
    sadness so deep
    one could know
    one could find
    tears that flow
    joy to seep
    through
    the mind
    the pain
    the fear
and then it shut

THEY SAY

grieve, they say
     what could have been
     will never be

let go, they say
     better is coming
     if you can believe
     this was a taste
     nothing a waste

surrender, they say
     wait for another door
     something good is in store

SUDDENLY

everything happened
everything changed
      in the eighth month
      of the first year

the love you had
the signs you showed

      hit a mark

           suddenly

                                        it all

                                        went

                                        dark

WHY

dream dashed
thriving crashed
broken heart
      missing
you who were
a best friend

now it breaks
all over again

     asking
     why

BEHIND A CLOSED DOOR

heart
torn out

hope
worn down

left
broken open
behind
a closed door

left
wanting
        more

WEEPING WILLOW

cry at night
out of sight
no one to see
or ask why
what's wrong

just me alone

      tears falling
      silently calling
      why, how long
      to the One
      who is there
      day and night

      never leaving
      always cleaving
      never deceiving
      always believing

cry it out
on the pillow
lose the doubt
leave the fear
weeping willow

you draw near
stay right here
the best is set
the best is yet

DOOR OF HOPE

Valley of Achor
desert of trouble
buried in rubble
pull me out
pull me up
away from the wild
     well watered
away from the war
     well waged
away from the wind
protected and planted
stable and strong
no longer lost
     tossed
blown or thrown
rooted and ready
secure and steady
take what I have
hold my hand
lead me out
lead me up
where light beams
     down
     down
on the door

See Beyond

Grieving seasons leave us feeling tossed around by
circumstances, emotions, and what or whom we miss.

In those times, how has God restored your hope?

Afterword

Wherever you are on your journey, I hope you learn to see beyond. May your faith deepen, your perspective grow, and your heart know –

God
moves mountains
meets us in
the valley
makes a way through
the desert
strengthens us in
storms

breaks barriers
builds bridges

loves to redeem
bring beauty
heal us in areas
we didn't know
needed
healing

May you be strong enough to face your limits, name your longings, learn to love, and learn to find hope after loss.

May you choose courage to go through the grieving season and say goodbye to what or whom you lost.

May you watch the people in your community show up and show how much they care. They will lend you strength, let you speak, and lead you to see glimpses of Hope scattered in your story.

May you continue to learn what it looks like to move beyond and how to thrive in every season of life.

Laura

Acknowledgments

I am grateful for everyone who has walked into my story
for a season, several years, or since I was born. The ones I
lost and the ones still here, I carry you close to my heart.

I wouldn't be who I am today without you.
I couldn't have written this book without you.

A simple thank you never feels like enough.
A special thank you goes to the following.

Mom, Dad, Raymond, and Phillip, thanks for teaching me
to see beyond from the beginning. Your unconditional love
and acceptance shaped my perspective. Your presence
helped me to become. Kaitlin and Ann, I gained sisters as
you joined our family.

Anna, you were the first friend to extend true hospitality.
And you were the first to envision the reality of this poetry
book. Thanks for always making me feel welcomed, seen,
and known for twenty-five years and counting.

Alyssa and Rachel, I nicknamed you my "little sisters." I'm
so glad God brought you both into my life when He did.
Thanks for making me laugh, sharing in adventures,
pointing me to Truth, and reminding me to be.

Allison, you brought me freedom and joy when you
stepped into my world. Thanks for expanding my own

understanding of how I view life and showing me new ways to do independence.

Janell and Will, the team behind the scenes. Janell, you are part counselor, editor, guide, and friend. You shine a light on my path, renewing my peace and strength to persevere to the next thing or season. Will, you use your gifts to keep me straight, help me ponder logistics for my ideas, and keep my site looking great and going strong.

Libby, Rosa, and Tasha, the mentors who listen and let me share in person or simply through a quick text or email. You brighten my days and remind me to hope. Thanks for your wisdom, encouragement, and prayers over the years.

Kathleen, Emily, and Kelly, we have stayed connected since we left Longwood and we find ways to meet up, catch up, and grow our friendship even more. Thanks for being three of the few I will call on the phone. I fondly treasure the college season with you and all the others.

Michelle, Luke, Sarah, Brian, Sarah, Marshall, Caleb, Jess, Levi, Ethan, you bless me beyond words at times. Wherever and whenever we gather, you invite me into your lives as I invite you into mine. I feel at home around all of you. Being a part of the same community is the best.

Summer Institute on Theology and Disability, you taught me community can be found anywhere, even on the road. Abby, Kirsty, Zach, Justin, and Lisa, we were instant friends and the impact you had on my life was deep and lasting. Thank you. I know I'll see you again somewhere.

And most importantly, God, you've been writing my story all along. I have learned to trust – you provide in every season and you do more than I could ever imagine.

About the Author

Laura C. Robb was born with Arthrogryposis Multiplex Congenita (AMC), a physical disability. Limitations have always affected her daily life, but she doesn't see obstacles. She sees these limits as opportunities for depending on God and her community.

Laura constantly finds ways to embrace the story she is living, chasing dreams and overcoming the challenges as they come. As she shares her own journey, Laura hopes to encourage others that thriving beyond limits is possible.

Connect with Laura on social media –

Instagram: @LauraCRobb
Facebook: @LauraCRobbWriter
Twitter: @LauraCRobb

Follow her blog, where she writes regularly about her experience of living with a disability –

LauraCRobb.com